# Stop Panic A

## *Easily & Forever*

*An easy-to-follow, step-by-step process to stop panic attacks*

*From a personal experience*

*Everything you need in one little book*

## © Copyright 2021 - All rights reserved.

*The content contained within this book may not be reproduced, duplicated, or transmitted without direct written permission from the author or the publisher.*

*Under no circumstances will any blame or legal responsibility be held against the publisher, or author, for any damages, reparation, or monetary loss due to the information contained within this book. Either directly or indirectly. You are responsible for your own choices, actions, and results.*

## Legal Notice:

*This book is copyright protected. This book is only for personal use. You cannot amend, distribute, sell, use, quote or paraphrase any part, or the content within this book, without the consent of the author or publisher.*

## Disclaimer Notice:

*Please note the information contained within this document is for educational and entertainment purposes only. All effort has been executed to present accurate-to-date, and reliable, complete information. No warranties of any kind are declared or implied. Readers acknowledge that the author is not engaging in the rendering of legal, financial, medical, or professional advice. The content within this book has been derived from various sources. Please consult a licensed professional before attempting any techniques outlined in this book.*

*By reading this document, the reader agrees that under no circumstances is the author responsible for any losses, direct or indirect, which are incurred as a result of the use of the information contained within this document, including, but not limited to, — errors, omissions, or inaccuracies.*

# Table of Contents

Introduction ............................................................. 9

Your story .............................................................. 13

My Story ............................................................... 15

Understanding is 90% of the fix ................................ 27

What's going on ..................................................... 31

Feelings ................................................................ 38

The light bulb moment! ........................................... 43

Look at what you now know! .................................... 48

Actions ................................................................. 49

Maintenance .......................................................... 54

Family & Friends .................................................... 61

Troubleshooting ..................................................... 63

A message from the author ...................................... 64

KIERA SCOTT

# Introduction

Congratulations, you've already taken the first step to complete freedom from panic attacks by buying this book. What you're about to learn is what a panic attack really is, and how you can easily stop them forever. Once you've read the book and taken a few simple steps, you'll never need to suffer again.

I want to thank you for trusting me with something that I know is unbelievably difficult for you, I know what you're going through because I've been exactly where you are now! I'm not a writer, this is the first book I've ever written, but I wanted to write it for you, and for every other person who is suffering unnecessarily from the hell of panic attacks.

This book comes from my real-life experience of living with multiple crippling panic attacks every day for many years, attacks that were so severe I could barely live my life, and I truly believed I would have no choice but to "manage" or "cope" with them every day, for the rest of my life.

Please trust me when I say, this is not the case, in this book
I will share with you how I finally stopped panic attacks easily and permanently, without help or medication, and how you can do exactly the same as I did!

I want to tell you what I've learned, and what I've shared with many others to help them do the same.

It's easy, with a logical, basic understanding and a few easy steps, that's all it takes, and it's fast, you can do this today, as soon as you finish reading this book, you'll quickly be back to who you used to be, living your life free from the fear of the next panic attack!

And once it's done, it's done, it doesn't matter how long you've suffered, how many panic attacks you've had, how severe they are, or your belief about what "triggers" them, this is permanent, and unfailingly works every time.

You'll soon be feeling complete joy when you realize that your panic hell is over, you'll never need to avoid social situations again or plan your life to accommodate panic attacks, and you'll be free from worrying, managing, or ever having panic attacks again!

## Tried & Tested

What you are about to read, wasn't always in book form, I've helped a lot of brave people who were living with panic attacks just like you for many years before I put everything into the final book, everyone I have previously helped has gone through exactly the same understanding and steps you are about to.

All I asked of them was that they listened to what I was telling them and follow the simple steps I will show you, some of them did it right away, some took a little longer, and some had the odd glitch along the way and started over.

Without exception, every single person who has followed the steps has had complete success and stopped panic attacks forever!

I continue to hear heart-warming stories from people I have helped who went on to help others who they knew were also suffering from panic disorder.

It makes me smile to know that they are sharing this information to help others, that each and every one of them are so grateful for the knowledge which allowed them to stop panic attacks forever, and that you are about to do the same.

Don't just take my word for it, I've asked some of them to share some feedback for the book...

## *Darren McIntyre*

"This is the answer, 100% blew me away. Makes so much sense. I did it! I am eternally grateful."

## *Kelly Shaw*

"After living with panic attacks for over 10 years my nightmare is over. I can't thank you enough. It's gone, completely gone in days."

## *Sean Timmons*

"I can't explain the feeling, I had suffered from panic for so long that I thought I could never change it. Within 3 days I was a new guy!"

# Your story

Everyone has a very different experience with panic attacks, and your experience will be individual to you. What I want to tell you first of all, is that you're exactly the same person you always were, you're just lost in this panic hell, but you can be completely free of it, and you will be soon.

I know it feels like something that nobody else is going through, and something that nobody else could possibly understand, you probably wouldn't even know how to explain it if you tried, but you're not alone I promise you that. Too many people are suffering like you are, and I know through my personal experience that all of you can be completely free from the hell of panic attacks.

You're probably apprehensive, and you're likely resigned to the belief that you need to just get on and cope with panic attacks, but what you are about to read will show you that you can stop these panic attacks forever, and never need to feel this way again. I will tell you some facts that may surprise you because you've been led to believe that you are stuck with this, I promise you it's not the case, you can and will conquer this, and I know you will.

Take your time with the book and re-read anything that you need to, the steps I took, and the steps you are about to take will change your life completely and allow you to live panic free forever!

Can you imagine a future where you feel like this forever? Now imagine a future where you never need to feel like this again!

# My Story

I wrote this book or the very first draft of it around 2011/2012, it then lived in a box in the loft to be uncovered again in 2020 when I was clearing out during the first Covid lockdown, anything to keep busy.

I completely forgot I had written it, and at the time of writing it I certainly didn't think I would publish it; I think I just wanted to get my thoughts, and my experience out of my head and down on paper, but whatever the reason, I was so glad I had found it.

After reading over what I had written I knew instantly that I should try to get it out there so that other people could benefit from it, so in my spare time I tweaked it here and there, trying to be as clear as possible, and finally finished it in late 2022.

Everything in this book is 100% from the heart, I know how horrific panic disorder is and I hope this book gives you exactly what it's intended to, complete peace from panic attacks.

As I said previously, everyone has a different experience with panic disorder, what you are about to read is my experience. This book is for you, it's not about me, so I've tried to keep it as condensed as possible. What I want to do in this chapter is to give you an understanding of the complete mess I was in, and the panic-driven life I was "living", it's to help you understand that if I can do this, then anyone can do this.

It was October 2006 and completely out of the blue I had my first panic attack, it was a whopper! I was driving in rush hour, city traffic and suddenly I just felt terrible, I was in a line of traffic and couldn't pull in, so I slowly crawled to and through the next set of traffic lights and pulled in at the side of the road.

It was the most terrifying, overwhelming feeling, like nothing I had ever felt before, my head was pounding, I had sensations running through my body, and I was convinced I was seriously ill, I felt like I was going to pass out or die! Terrified, I sat at the side of the road wondering what the hell was going on, I phoned my husband and tried to explain to him, but he was working and couldn't get to me, I must have terrified him, I was freaking out and making no sense.

Eventually, things calmed down a bit and the overwhelming feeling left, however, I still felt terrible from it, and my head was still thumping. I sat there for a while trying to work out what was going on, and wondering if I would be able to drive at all. After sitting there for about 15 minutes I decided to try to drive the rest of the way home, I chose the best route home to ensure I had an opportunity to pull the car into the side of the road if I felt unwell again.

This was the start of my route-planning hell which lasted until I stopped driving completely!

As I continued my journey home all I could think about was how I was feeling, and when I felt like I couldn't drive anymore, I pulled the car in until I got myself together and drove for another section of the journey home. That 15-minute journey took me over an hour that day, stopping and starting along the way, always ensuring I was taking the route that allowed me to pull the car in.

I arrived home and drove into the driveway, by this time my head was really thumping. I went into the house and went straight upstairs to lie down on my bed, I didn't even say hello to my family I just felt so ill, I had to lie down. My husband came upstairs to see me when he came home, but I couldn't explain it to him, I just wanted to lie there quietly until I felt better, the headache lasted for hours, and I felt so shaken and drained.

That was the first panic attack I ever had! Why? What triggered it? I'll explain that a little later in the book.

The next day I was on my way to work, and it happened again, this time in the fuel station when I was filling the car. I sat in the car in tears, I phoned my doctor and booked an appointment, the quickest she could see me was 2 days later, 2 days seemed like the longest time, I wanted to curl up in a ball and wait to see her.

When I arrived at work another panic attack struck me, at the time I worked in a city college with long corridors when the panic attack hit me, I was in the corridor and the sensation was terrifying, I honestly can't explain it to this day, it was like being in a horror movie. My boss found me freaking out in the corridor and sent me home. I have no idea why I told her I was fine to get myself home, why do we say we're fine when clearly, we're not?

It took me another hour to drive back home, constantly stopping and starting and planning my route to make sure I could stop.

I didn't go out for the 2 days before seeing the doctor, I couldn't even go to work, and the utter fear of it happening again completely took over. By the time I saw the doctor I had spent so much time on Google, I was telling her what I had the symptoms of.
She was so very patient with me and tested me for everything she felt may help her work out what was wrong, she sent me home and told me to take some time off and rest, I made an appointment to return in 5 days for test results.

The 5-day wait was filled with one panic attack after another, things seemed to be getting worse every day, and I was convinced that there was something seriously wrong with me.

When I went back to the doctor's surgery, she was looking at me with sympathetic eyes, as she told me that all my tests were good and that there was no reason to be concerned about my health.

She then went on to suggest that I was having panic attacks, I thought she was mad, the only thing I knew, or "thought" I knew about panic attacks was that you would feel short of breath, and a bit stressed, how wrong was I! I told her that she must be wrong and that it was so much more than that, I thought this couldn't possibly be panic attacks, I believed I was seriously ill. I left the doctor's surgery, went home, and cried.

From then things just got worse every day, and by the end of November I wouldn't drive at all, I barely went out, I was terrified all the time, there was a constant feeling of utter dread in the pit of my stomach, and I spent my days with one thought in my head "how do I feel?". By this time, I was having around 10 – 12 whopping panic attacks every day, I couldn't function. I didn't believe it was panic that was causing me to feel this way, I was convinced my doctor, and the doctors and nurses in A&E were missing something.

Yes, I had various visits to A&E and my doctor, that's how bad it was, and each time they would tell me I was having panic attacks and I should consider various therapies, etc. my doctor would suggest something prescribed to help with the symptoms, and I would refuse, because in my head there must have been something seriously wrong with me, there was no way this could be panic.

What I was feeling was physical, I would feel completely outside of myself, almost fuzzy, I would feel strange warm feelings coming over me, my legs would seize my body ached and sometimes twitched, I had skull-crushing headaches, and I would get pins and needles anywhere and everywhere on my body, but I never had the feeling of shortness of breath which was the only thing I "thought" I knew about panic attacks. Nobody could convince me that this was panic disorder!

One day comes to mind when I think of A&E, one afternoon I was so unwell with it all, it was probably one of the worst days of my life. I was at home, of course, but the entire day had been filled with one panic attack after another, my head and neck were so sore and I felt like my ear was closing over, as though I was getting an infection or something.

As the day went on my entire body was reacting, my arms and legs seemed nearly numb, and I felt lightheaded all day. Eventually, it got so bad I asked my husband to drive me to A&E. He was really worried about me, I could see it in his eyes, which terrified me even more, I was convinced I was going to the hospital to hear terrible news.

We drove to A&E, which is literally 5 minutes from our house, but when we got there, I couldn't get out of the car, my legs wouldn't work, and I couldn't feel them, I mean absolutely no sensation whatsoever, I was completely overwhelmed and sat sobbing in the car, terrified. Eventually, I managed to swing my legs around and get out of the car, leaning on my husband for physical and mental support I made my way into A&E. The sight of me barely holding my own body weight must have alerted the receptionist who instantly appeared with a wheelchair and called someone to take me straight through.

After some time and various tests, I was told once again that I may have been suffering panic attacks, and the sympathetic nurse sent me on my way. I remember leaving the hospital that day, not feeling relieved that I wasn't seriously ill, but instead feeling completely beaten down, drained, and seeing no way out of the hell I was living.

Over the years I spoke with so many doctors, health professionals, and counsellors who always tried to convince me that I was suffering from panic disorder, they were always kind and sympathetic as they sent me away with various suggestions, coping and management techniques, etc. none of which ever helped.

Worst of all the doctors would offer me pills to ease the symptoms, but what they failed to see was that the thought of taking the pills for the rest of my life just sent me into another downward spiral, it was a vicious circle that I could see no way out of.

As the months went by, I adjusted my entire life to accommodate the panic attacks, missing family gatherings, and missing days out with my husband and sons, I didn't drive again for 5 years, I sold my car and my poor ever loving husband had to chauffeur me around, well he didn't have to, but he did because he's amazing and just wanted to see me well.

On top of everything I was trying to keep my "condition" away from my boys, I didn't want them to worry about me, I felt so lost, and I didn't want them to see that. It was impossible to make plans because if I did make plans and then feel bad on the day, I would need to cancel and let people down, which made me feel bad again.

My safe place was home, and I stayed there as often as I could. I missed so many days and nights out, weekends away, and social gatherings, and if I did go, I would need to overcompensate and force a smile to get me through it, still feeling awful inside. I associated so many things and situations with the possibility of feeling that way, so I avoided life.

I'm lucky to have the friends I have, they may never know how much I appreciate them sticking around, even though I couldn't explain how I was feeling, and for that, I am eternally grateful, they know who they are.

As the years went by this was my new normal, I'm not sure I could even remember the person I used to be before panic disorder stepped in. I was tired, I was overly emotional, I was difficult to live with, life was difficult, and I was scared all the time. I believed that I was ill, and nobody could tell me what was wrong, I was exhausted and just trying to get through the next hour.

12th May 2011, 9.30 am, my husband and 2 sons were going out for the day, I couldn't go with them as I was having a "bad day", I had a panic attack about an hour earlier and I was feeling awful. I said goodbye from the top of the stairs as my legs felt like they would hardly hold me to get down and back up the stairs, I was so drained.

When I say that now it seems a world away, but there were many days when my body just wouldn't work properly due to the sensations of panic disorder, it really was horrific.

When the boys left for the day, everything really hit me, completely overwhelmed me, and I sat at the top of the stairs in tears, tired of missing life, and exhausted from the effort and strength it took to get through each day. As I sat there in pieces, I knew things had to change, I couldn't go on like this, I had read so many books and listened to so many people telling me that this was with me for life and that I would need to manage it day to day, but that wasn't an option for me, it couldn't be the only way.

I walked into my son's room, and his laptop was lying open on his bed, I googled "panic attacks", and I started to read various articles on panic attacks and how to "manage them", mostly medicinal which just didn't suit me, the thought of taking medicine every day for the rest of my life just sent me into a tailspin. Every article seemed to suggest that I had to accept and manage it, there wasn't anything on how to stop them.

I called my doctor and got a same-day appointment, she was pleased to see me and even more pleased that I wanted to discuss the possibility that I was having panic attacks, we discussed things at length, and she did a general health check for me, however, she couldn't direct me or tell me anything about stopping panic attacks permanently. She told me that I could manage them with tablets and see if that helped, it just seemed like a waste of time being there.

I get it, she's a doctor and her years of medical training tells her that she should prescribe something for it, but it just didn't sit well with me, I knew it couldn't be the only way to go, but I left with a prescription for both anti-depressants and Valium. I went to the chemist on the way home and picked them up, when I got home, I sat on the sofa drained from yet another day of managing and coping with panic attacks.

I looked at the prescription drugs the doctor had prescribed me, but instead of looking forward to their effect on the panic attacks, I was overwhelmed with the fear of relying on prescription medication every day, and of course, I had another panic attack!

I spent the rest of that day online, researching panic attacks, and researching natural remedies, this was one step away from prescription medication and it still seemed to imply that panic attacks needed to be managed and coped with, there really was no information at all on stopping them forever.

After many hours of reading, I closed the laptop and ran a hot bath. As I lay in the bath playing things over in my head from what I had read that day, I noticed that so much of the information I was reading was saying that panic is caused by the fear of it, nothing more, and all of a sudden, I had the thought, "so if I don't fear it, then it won't happen?" Surely it can't be that simple!

I lay quietly in the bath for a while and then got out, and dried. As I sat down on my bed, I felt a panic attack starting, instantly I thought "don't be scared or you'll feed it" I slowed my panicking thoughts the best I could, dropped my shoulders, took a breath, and said, "don't feed the fear of this." Suddenly, the panic attack that was right there just stopped, and I don't mean it faded away the same way every other one had, I mean it stopped, completely stopped!

I felt so much happiness rushing in, but then I thought "was it really a panic attack, did I just think it was, did I really just stop it?" I think I was so beaten down by the years of panic, I didn't trust my own judgment. I went to bed that night wondering if I really had just stopped that panic attack, or was I imagining it?

13th May 2011, 10.15 am the day everything changed! 24 hours previously I was sitting at the top of my staircase, a shell of the person I had been before, and now I was driving without a care in the world!

I know the exact time because I remember looking at the dashboard clock and thinking "24 hours ago I was broken" I smiled a smile from my soul, the relief I felt and the utter joy was unexplainable, I just knew it was over.

I hardly went home that day; I went to a supermarket alone for the first time in years, I walked the dogs more times than they wanted, and I went for a walk on my own which I hadn't done in years! I never had another panic attack that day, and I've never had another one since.

Later in the book, I will explain exactly what I did that day, and it's exactly the same as you will do but we need to give you an understanding of panic attacks before you take the same steps I did, you need to understand why the steps work before you can take them but for now, just know that's how quick it was for me, and that's how quick it can be for you!

# Understanding is 90% of the fix

Understanding what is going on is 90% of what you need to stop panic attacks forever, it's that simple.

This book will take you from where you are now with your disordered thoughts and beliefs, to a clearer understanding of what is actually happening, and this will allow you to take the few simple steps to have total peace from panic attacks. Currently, your thoughts and beliefs are "disordered", and this can make it very difficult for you to see or believe anything beyond what the doctors and health professionals have told you, so first I need to ask you to let go of everything you believe and everything you have ever been told about panic attacks.

Clearly, nothing you have tried in the past has worked otherwise you wouldn't need this book, so let go of all of it, none of it has done you any real good or harm, so let it go.

I have kept the following chapters as simple as possible, in order not to overwhelm you with unhelpful facts and information, your only aim is to stop the panic attacks fast, you don't need chapter after chapter of examples and so on, as none of this helps.

## Myth Busting

Before we go any further, let's bust some myths...

You probably think you need to learn how to "manage" panic attacks to live day to day but that's completely wrong.

You can, and with the help of this book, will irradicate panic disorder from your life easily and forever! This book will change your total belief, and once you know, you know!

---

You probably think you're ill, but that's also completely wrong, although panic attacks are extremely frightening, they're not at all dangerous, you're not ill.

A panic attack will not cause you any physical harm, and it's very unlikely you'd be admitted to the hospital if you have one.

You probably think that it's only weak people who have panic attacks, but that's also completely wrong! Only strong people can live their lives coping with panic attacks day in, and day out!

You're so much stronger than you believe.

---

You probably think panic attacks are caused by triggers, but this is also completely wrong.

The only thing that triggers a panic attack in any situation is your heightened state of anxiety, feeding the fear, and focusing on how you feel!

---

*Energy flows where your attention goes. If you think about it, believe something triggers it, or hold it in your mind as your predominant thought, it will show up for you, every time, without fail!*

Before you started having panic attacks, like me you probably believed that it was some sort of shortness of breath brought on by a stressful situation, but that's not true at all!

You do not need medication or specialist help **It is vital that you talk to your doctor before reducing or stopping any medication you are currently taking** discuss what is in this book with your doctor and they will happily support you along the road of reducing and or stopping any medication.

# What's going on

### What is panic?

Panic happens to everyone, it's natural, and helpful when there is something to panic about, and most people settle back down again to a normal, calmer level and move on from whatever caused them to panic, this is how you used to react before panic disorder arrived in your life and changed everything, a totally natural reaction, fight or flight.

Fight or flight is something we all have hard-wired into our brain from the days of the caveman, learning to recognize fear and running, or fighting to survive in everyday life, we need it to keep us safe in dangerous situations.

### What is panic disorder?

You will see me say panic disorder throughout this book, the word disorder will help you understand that currently, your beliefs are "disordered", and you need to "reorder" them. What you will learn in this book will help you to reorder your thoughts and beliefs.

Panic disorder is when you suffer from panic attacks and constantly worry and adapt your routine to avoid having another one.

When you suffer from panic disorder you have a constant feeling of unease, or dread which can range from mild to severe, you feel terrified and overwhelmed even though you are in no danger at all. Your brain can't find a logical explanation for it, so you get scared, the fear builds, and boom you have a panic attack. Panic disorder is the most severe form of anxiety.

Understanding how you have ended up with panic disorder isn't difficult, after a culmination of challenging circumstances, either after years or sometimes months, weeks, or even days, you have set your anxiety level to a constant high alert and it's sitting right there, reacting on cue when the circumstances are right, it takes barley anything to set a panic attack in motion because your anxiety level is already extremely high.

You don't even notice that you are in a constant anxious state because it's your normal, and you just carry on.

When you look back over your life, you may see that you've always felt anxious inside for who knows what reason or you had an anxious parent and learned what you saw, or a bad relationship that had you tied up in knots and you've never been the same since, trauma of any sort, bereavement, the list is endless.

The important thing to know is that none of this matters, why does it matter if you realize that you first had a panic attack 5 years ago when you suffered a tragedy or a life-changing event? Why does it matter if your parent is anxious, and you've learned the same behaviour? Can we ever really know, do we need to link it to something? Why, would that help? No, it wouldn't, don't look to blame an event or person, it's a waste of time, it will just tie you up in knots and can't possibly help you move on.

Around 3% of adults in the UK have it, and it's more common in women than in men. Children can also suffer from panic disorder.

## What is a panic attack?

When you feel a panic attack, what you are feeling is fear, that's all it is, just fear! It's the feeling of undirected fear.

It's when you suddenly feel panic for no apparent reason, it feels like a rush of intense mental and/or physical symptoms. It feels as though it is taking over, you feel as though it's in control, and it feels as though you can't stop it. When you have a heightened state of anxiety (panic disorder) it takes nothing at all to set off a panic attack.

When you feel fear because of imminent danger, you know why you are feeling the fear, your logical brain can attach it to the dangerous situation, it makes sense, you understand it, and when the danger passes everything calms down and you go on with your day.

The problem is when you're having a panic attack the fear is there for no apparent reason, so you can't logically attach it to anything, it's undirected fear, you don't understand why you're feeling this panic, and there's no reason for it, it freaks you out, it's absolutely terrifying and your fear feeds the fear, sending you into a tailspin.

A panic attack cannot hurt you; it is nothing! I can't emphasize this enough, a panic attack is absolutely nothing, it's equal to feeling hot, cold, itchy, or ticklish, it's just a sensation, or sometimes a few sensations all at the one time, but that's all it is, fear is just a sensation.

If our temperature was too low, our brain would send us the sensation of cold and we would put a sweater on. If we are itchy our brain sends us the sensation and we scratch the itch. It's just sensations, nothing to fear.

Don't look for a reason why you started having panic attacks, just accept you do and move on to stopping them.

It doesn't matter how long you have panicked, what you attribute panicking to, how many panic attacks you've had, where, and when panic attacks happen. This is all just the story you've been telling yourself.

A panic attack can last anywhere from 1 to 10 minutes, but it can linger and continue to make you feel awful for hours.
You are not in any physical danger, at all, ever!

There is no minimum or maximum amount you will have, it may be 1 per week, day, or hour.

One in 10 adults in the U.K. have a panic attack each year and they usually begin between the ages of 13 and 30.

About a third of people have one in their lifetime, but most of them don't have panic disorder.

## What triggers a panic attack?

Nothing triggers a panic attack, your thoughts and beliefs are disordered you're set to a constant heightened state of anxiety, and you fear having a panic attack, which brings it on and feeds it until you have a panic attack. (Panic disorder)

No situation causes a panic attack, you may find yourself in a situation and believe it's going to bring on a panic attack, and then you have a panic attack but that's not because of the situation, it's because you were terrified of having a panic attack, and the fear of the fear brought the fear.

You associate panic attacks with an event and convince yourself it's a trigger i.e. I have panic attacks when I drive, or when I'm in a lift/elevator, or when I'm left alone.

All of these "reasons" or "triggers" are you trying to link the panic attack to an event or circumstance because you can't believe that this horrendous feeling would happen for no reason at all.

It's also the reason you attach panic attacks to being ill, it's more logical for you to believe you're unwell, as you believe you couldn't possibly feel this way if you were well.

I had my first panic attack in my car and therefore attached having panic attacks to driving and didn't drive again for years.

This is what happens, this is an attempt at making sense of it all, so we convince ourselves it must be a trigger and we start to avoid circumstances and events before we know it our entire life spirals into panic hell!

Whatever it is that you believe "causes" the panic attack, it's vital to understand that this is just a belief, and you are in total control of reordering that belief.

You've managed to talk yourself into this, now let's talk yourself out of it.

**Here's a list of the "triggers" I believed, it's no wonder I had no life...**

Driving

Socializing

Planes, trains, and automobiles

Subways

Shops

Washing my hair (that one does make me laugh)

# Feelings

Imagine you walk off the pavement into the moving traffic, a car sounds its horn, and you jump back onto the pavement to safety, for a moment your heart is pounding, and you feel the fear, you realize you're fine and you settle back down before attempting to cross the road more safely this time.

Well, that's it, that feeling of fear when you jump at the sound of the car horn, people who suffer from panic disorder feel that same level of stress and fear all the time, they just don't recognize it because it's always with them, and when the situation is right, they get tipped over the edge into utter panic!

**Symptoms/Sensations**

Where to begin? First, everyone I have ever helped, researched, or spoken to about panic attacks has had a different experience, some feel it physically, some feel it in their gut which makes them feel sick, some feel it mentally and some feel a combination of all.

Whatever you feel, I know it's horrendous for you, but I promise you we will soon change that.

## What you might feel

Feeling like you are going to pass out

Feeling like you are outside of your body

Feeling fuzzy

Feelings of utter dread

Feeling sick

Headaches

Sweating or Chills

Racing heartbeat

Short of breath

Pains in your chest

Pains anywhere

Pins & Needles

Shaking

Hot flushes

Choking

Numbness

And that's only the beginning, there are many more, but they are all one and the same, it's your body reacting to the fear. It doesn't matter what symptoms you have, what you are learning here in this book will work for you.

You are not ill; you don't need to get better! This is good news, you will be amazed at how many ailments leave you once you stop panic attacks, things you had never linked to panic attacks will just disappear!

I suffered from aches and pains for years, I had constant headaches, and my memory was terrible. Once I stopped the panic attacks, I felt lighter, my body wasn't aching anymore, the headaches were completely gone, and my memory was sharper than it had ever been.

You see I had been holding so much stress in my muscles for so many years my body reacted to it, and just ached all the time, and the headaches were caused by the stress in my neck, shoulders, and back. As soon as I stopped the panic attacks all of this went, overnight, it just left me, and I felt like a new woman.

It's just a feeling, feelings are not real, nothing is happening, just let it go.

## Resistance

> *"What you resist persists."*
>
> *Carl Jung*

The phrase "what you resist persists" means that when you resist or fight against something, it can actually make that thing stronger or more persistent. This can apply to a variety of situations, such as personal struggles, social issues, or even physical sensations.

For example, if you are trying to overcome fear, constantly resisting, or avoiding that fear may actually reinforce it and make it more difficult to overcome.

In essence, the phrase suggests that acceptance and non-resistance are more effective in resolving issues than active resistance or fighting. By accepting a situation and understanding it, you will be better equipped to address it positively, rather than perpetuating it through resistance.

Everyone in the world experiences resistance, resistance is something you will have felt throughout your life, it's a natural response to changes, challenges, and discomfort, basically, a protective mechanism that helps you stay within your comfort zone, however, resistance can also hold you back.

One way it can hold you back is by adding to fear, this can prevent you from taking action when you need to or trying new things and stepping outside of your comfort zone. It can make you believe that you're not capable of succeeding, which further reinforces your resistance and limits your efforts.

Remember, resistance is a natural part of everyone's life, you won't ever get rid of it, everyone has it, not just you and not just people who suffer from panic disorder, but don't let it stop you.

Resistance will raise its ugly head and try to talk you out of just about anything, and more often than not it can be a sign that you're on the right track, for some unknown reason resistance works really hard trying to get you to avoid doing the most important things for you.

It's important to recognize when resistance is present, recognize what it's trying to sabotage, and then carry on regardless.

**Here are my top 3 strategies to help you beat resistance:**

Be aware of negative self-talk and beliefs which are adding to your resistance, it's just a story you're telling yourself, don't listen to it, and don't believe it.

Look for inspiration and motivation from sources that resonate with you, such as books, podcasts, or motivational speakers. Over the years I've read many books on understanding resistance, and if it's something you would be interested in learning more about then I must highly recommend one author, Steven Pressfield. You can find him at - stevenpressfield.com. Do the work, is probably one of the best books I have ever read on the subject, it's a book I still use often when resistance is showing up in my life.

Ultimately, the best way to beat resistance is to take action.

# The light bulb moment!

You will have a lightbulb moment, it's the moment when you realize you get it, you can feel it, you see it, you know it's all over and you won't ever need to suffer like that again. When it happens you will laugh inside, I want you to recognize that feeling and laugh out loud, when you finally see and feel that you have changed it instantly, I want you to laugh out loud and feel the utter joy of it!

My lightbulb moment came on Friday 13th May 2011, it still makes me laugh that it was Friday the 13th. I woke up around 7 am and my first thought as always was "how do I feel?". I actually felt ok that morning and as I lay there my mind went back to the previous evening, once again asking all the questions, "did a panic attack actually stop suddenly? that had never happened before, did it happen, or did I imagine it? was it even a panic attack? did I stop it? was I in control of this all along?" I could feel the same happiness from the evening before eating into my soul, and I could feel myself trying to smile about it, but unsure if I should, maybe I was wrong, maybe it wasn't a panic attack after all.

*Ah, the mind of a panic sufferer certainly is an overthinker.*

I wasn't working that day and hadn't made any plans, I got up, had a shower, got dressed, and went downstairs, I continued to think about the panic attack that had completely stopped the previous evening, "was it really as simple as not feeding the fear?" there was only one way to prove it to myself, I knew I had to be brave when the next panic attack arrived and try to stop it again.

I could easily have waited on a panic attack to arrive, as I was confident that one would show up sooner or later, but I didn't want to wait, for the first time in 5 years I wanted a panic attack to come so I could try to stop it, and yes it was a bit scary, but I knew I had to try. I thought to myself "how can I bring on a panic attack?"

My husband's car was in the driveway and the key was on the table, I was insured to drive it as he had kept my name on his insurance policy in the hope that one day I would drive again. I grabbed the key and went outside to the car, it took me a moment to open the car and sit in the driver's seat, I sat there feeling a bit overwhelmed after all this is where it had all begun for me. I hadn't driven in 5 years, and I could hear my resistant, panicking mind telling me no, it's not a good idea, but I knew I had to ignore it and just carry on. I started the engine and sat there for another few mins before reversing out of the driveway, I drove very slowly down the street which, to be honest terrified me the whole way, however, we live in a reasonably quiet estate, perfect for a first attempt at driving again.

I continued into the next street and the next and the next, by now I had been driving for a few mins and felt ok, a bit wobbly but ok. The next street was the main road and as I approached the junction, I felt a panic attack coming and it was coming fast, the car was already stationary as I was waiting on the traffic clearing so I could pull out onto the main road. I took a breath and felt myself allowing the panic attack to come, I dropped my shoulders and welcomed it, I didn't feed it with fear, I just calmly allowed it to come, I say calmly but obviously, nobody is calm when a panic attack is starting, what I mean by calmly is, I tried to stay as calm as possible rather than going into full-on "oh s**t" mode like I usually would.

Right there and then as the panic started to build I tried to see if I could control it, but I didn't try to calm it down, I tried to make it worse, and while I was focusing on trying to make it worse, to my astonishment it just stopped, it had gone, I mean it stopped in seconds, as soon as I focused on trying to make it worse, suddenly it was completely gone, just like the previous evening!

I tried to bring it back, but it just wouldn't come back, I drove for at least an hour trying to trigger another, but it just wouldn't happen, eventually, I stopped the car at the side of the road, and I laughed at myself in the rear-view mirror.

I couldn't believe what was happening, I had experienced 10 to 12 panic attacks just the day before and every day before that for the previous 5 years, and now it was gone. I cannot explain the instant relief I felt in my neck, shoulders, and entire body, my head was light and all I could feel was an ease that I hadn't felt in such a long time.

I spent most of that day driving and going out and about, I didn't want to go home and waste the feeling, I felt exhilarated.

I hadn't driven a car or had this level of independence in 5 years, it was amazing, and I felt completely free. I have never had another panic attack to this day, and I know I can't have another one because I completely get it, I completely understand the logic of it, and I no longer feed the fear.

## What did I do that day?

Well, I had to be a little bit brave, I just knew I had to do this or live in the hell of panic forever, so I welcomed it, I just let it come without tensing up, freaking out, or feeding it with my fear. I played with it to prove to myself that I was in control, and as soon as I felt that I was in total control of it, it just went away.

That's it, that's all I did and that's what you are going to do soon.

The actions you will take are basic and easy, but I promise you this is all you need to do, you just need to prove to yourself that you are in complete control, and it will be gone, forever!

Your belief will switch instantly, and without effort, your panic level will reduce to a normal level, and because you can see it and feel it happening to you when it does switch, you'll know it.

Your new understanding of panic disorder will give you the freedom to deal with it easily, once and for all, and you can get back to living your life panic free.

# Look at what you now know!

Now you have a full understanding of what a panic attack really is, and why they make you feel the way you do. You know there is nothing to be afraid of, it's just sensations, and you know sensations can't hurt you in any way. You know you're not ill, and you know that this can be dealt with easily.

I know it's a little bit scary, but the most important things in life require us to be brave. Listen to what this book is telling you and trust me, please trust me, just try it and your life will change.

I promise you this works so fast, and it's so easy, you just need to trust yourself for a minute or less during the next panic attack, and that's it, it's all gone, for good.

Please stop for a moment, take a deep breath, and feel yourself exhaling all those incorrect beliefs and tensions you have been carrying around unnecessarily for such a long time. Allow your shoulders to drop and know that you will never need to feel like this again.

Knowledge really is power!

# Actions

Now that you understand what's going on when you are having panic attacks, and you know there is nothing at all to fear, it's time to take a few simple steps and stop panic attacks forever.

It's time to live again! No more missing out on life! No more feeling overwhelmed and exhausted.

Let go of all the false beliefs you have about panic attacks, and all the worry and stress you felt about them, you now know that they are absolutely nothing to fear, and you can deal with them easily, once and for all.

You're the only one who can create the panic-free life you deserve.

There are 3 steps below and a few hints and tips to help you along the way. All you need to do is follow the steps.

Trust me and trust yourself, let's go...

**Step 1. Be Brave**

Being brave doesn't mean you're not afraid, it means you're willing to face your fears and take action anyway. I believe in you, and I know you have what it takes to overcome this. I bet you've faced tough situations before and come out stronger, and you can do it again.

I hope everything we've discussed so far has given you some peace of mind, and a good understanding that everything you have been feeling has just been sensations. Trust me, I know how you're feeling, I've been there, it's been a tough time for you, and I completely understand that. All I ask is that you take a breath, remove fear and doubt and be a little bit brave, you have nothing to lose and everything to gain. Don't listen to resistance telling you that you can't do this, you can, and you will.

**Step 2. Welcome the next panic attack**

Welcoming the feeling of fear or panic can be difficult, but it's an essential part of this process. When you recognize it, instead of judging it or trying to change it, just accept it for what it is, nothing more than a feeling. Rather than pushing the fear away or fighting it, try to sit with it and allow yourself to feel it fully, I know this sounds uncomfortable, but it's a very important step that will help to reduce resistance and create space for healing.

By welcoming and allowing fear or panic, you can begin to heal. When you experience fear your natural tendency is to push the feeling away, however, this can actually make the fear worse and keep you stuck in a cycle of avoidance and suppression.

When the next panic attack arrives, I want you to welcome it, don't be scared, remember it's just a sensation, it can do you absolutely no harm. Let it come and don't resist it, calm your fear, it's the fear that feeds it.

Be aware of the tension you are holding in your body, and drop your shoulders, releasing as much tension as you can. I know this will feel odd because your body is so used to reacting and fighting against a looming panic attack but do all you can to keep as calm as possible without resisting or feeding it with fear.

### Step 3. Play with the panic attack and see that you are in complete control of it

I want you to play with it, make it worse, if possible, I mean really be aware of it and feel yourself controlling it, it's not controlling you, and you will very quickly see and feel that it's you who's doing it.

Try calming it down, and as it does calm down, I want you to try to make it worse again. I want you to play with the panic attack to show yourself that you are in control of it. Don't fear it, it's nothing!

This will be your last ever panic attack. Test it, and try "triggering" another one, it won't happen because you understand the logic, and you can play with it! This works even better if you have a place or situation that you have always believed triggers panic attacks. Take yourself to that place and try to bring on a panic attack it just won't work, and even if you do feel one trying to brew then that's great, that's your opportunity to make it worse and play with it until you see once and for all that it's you who is in total control of it.

See it, feel that it's you who is controlling this sensation, and then you will know and believe that it's all over, this will be your lightbulb moment!

This is permanent, do this once and that's it, try to do it again if you don't believe me, it's impossible to bring on a panic attack from the moment you understand it and feel it, and know you are in total control of it!

It will never happen again, it's impossible, the logic you have learned just won't let it happen.

Now you know, you just know, you feel it, it makes perfect sense, you challenge it to prove it to yourself, and if the resistance in your head tries to trick you back into panicking, you challenge yourself again and free yourself forever, knowing what you know now, that you are in total control, the logic won't allow you to go backward, it's impossible, your mind can't go back to panicking again, because you understand it.

Stop giving up years of your life chasing every program, therapy session, or medication that "might" help you "cope". That just leaves it festering inside you for another day, while you hang on to the belief that you need to "manage" panic disorder.

This will work even if you don't believe it will., it needs to, your mind cannot argue with what it experiences, and when it experiences you beating it, it will retreat, and it will never happen again.

*If it didn't work for you the first time you try this, please don't worry, or be disheartened. It's just because you are hanging onto a bit of fear and uncertainty. Don't worry about it, you can do it again when you are ready.

# Maintenance

You might be wondering if there is any maintenance that needs to be done to keep you on track, the short answer is no, once you see and understand that you are controlling it, and rid yourself of them, that's it, you're done. Just live your life to the fullest, free from the crippling burden of panic disorder. You will never have another panic attack! How do I know? because your brain can't have undirected panic now, I know because you understand it, you know it's within your control to make them worse or irradicate them from your life altogether. So, what now?

**Focus on something new**

Find yourself a new focus, this one has ruled your life for long enough, this is a key element to supporting the new panic free you, it's such an important part of this.

A new focus will replace the space you have in your head, your brain needs stimulation and if the only thing you focus on is day-to-day life, kids, job, and anything that you have in your life, you leave so much space up there in your head that you don't know what to do with yourself, you get anxious, ratty, uncomfortable and that's when you don't feel mentally strong.

Is there something you have always wanted to learn? Learn it, everything is free online these days, or walk to the library, a completely underused resource these days I know, but without a doubt one of the most peaceful places to just sit and regroup. Just start reading articles, anything about whatever it is you want to learn.

This is your new focus, don't use it as a distraction, if you think of it as a distraction from panic disorder, then you are just thinking about panic and keeping it in your life, use it to build a new stronger version of yourself. Total focus on your new thing is what you need!

You know that moment in the morning, just for a few seconds when you wake up and you forget that you panic, just for a few seconds then it kicks in, that's because when you've been asleep, you are not giving any focus to panic, and waking up, your head is at peace for just a few seconds and then you start focusing on it again. But that little moment of respite the moment you open your eyes is what you will find when you totally immerse yourself in your new focus, you'll forget all about panic attacks.

## Meditation

Meditation is a very powerful tool that will help to improve your current anxious state, it will help to calm your mind and reduce your physiological responses to stress, which in turn will lead to a reduction in your anxiety and stress levels.

Regular meditation practice will help to regulate your emotions and increase your emotional resilience, allowing you to better manage difficult or challenging situations.

I highly recommend implementing meditation into your life, the benefits will astound you, you can practice meditation alone, or as part of a larger group, and should aim to meditate for around 10 to 15 minutes daily.

Or if you prefer you can just go for a walk every day on your own in the local park or along some quieter streets, don't be on the phone or listening to music or anything else, just be quiet, let any thoughts, good or bad just float by, don't hold onto them, just let it be some quiet time. Initially, your head will be busy and chatty but just let it pass, enjoy the peace, and settle your soul down.

I started meditating not long after I stopped having panic attacks, I use transcendental meditation but there are many ways to meditate, have a look online to see what options there are and find something that resonates with you.

Meditation practice has given me balance throughout my entire day, not just while I'm meditating, and my anxiety levels have been at an all-time low since I started.

## Visualization

Visualization is also a powerful tool for achieving personal goals, when you create a vivid mental image of how you want your life to be, it will increase your motivation and focus, and improve your chances of success.

Close your eyes and create a vivid mental image of yourself living a panic-free life, use all your senses to make it as realistic as possible, see and feel yourself as you used to be, or as you want to be now. Really feeling it, feeling the joy and normality of it, paying attention to all the details, can help to create a more immersive experience.

Don't think of it in the past tense, feel it now, and make believe you are already living the way you want to; it'll soon be a reality.

**Let it go**

Let it all go and don't be a victim, I cannot express how important this is.

Don't dwell on or talk about the "struggle" of panic disorder, the difficult event or circumstance that you believe is to blame for panic disorder, or tell your panic story repeatedly, it just keeps it with you.

I know this sounds harsh but please understand the damage that you can do to your mental health when you hang onto the story is immense.

What you need to do is talk about the freedom of moving on from this horrible time in your life and be proud that you have done this all on your own. Other panic sufferers will be inspired by your strength and ability to move on fully from panic disorder. Focus only on the positive aspects of your success, be positive about everything as you move on, don't blame people, circumstances, or events for the panic you felt, don't complain about how difficult it was, and don't justify any negativity by blaming panic disorder.

Just let it all go, be joyful that you are free, and move, it doesn't need to define you or control you anymore, just let it go.

## Educate others

When you educate someone else who is suffering from panic disorder, you will need to organize your own thoughts to be able to explain clearly and concisely, this will help you better understand the process yourself.

They may ask you questions or challenge what you are telling them, which will help solidify your own understanding even more. Overall, educating others can be a valuable tool for improving your own understanding, retention, and application of the information.

Telling people what you've achieved is one of the best feelings in the world, you'll feel proud of yourself, and quite right, you've been through a horrible experience, but you're free of it now, you know and understand the dark hole of panic disorder, and when you start to tell others how easily you overcame this and educate them about how they can do the same, the more you will cement the logic in your own mind, it'll help you and them.

Be careful not to focus on the woe-is-me version of the story, I know it's been a tricky time for you but hanging onto the negative will just bring negative experiences to you. I want you to focus on the joy of it, educate others by telling them how free you are, and how easy it was to achieve.

You'll be surprised how many people you know who are suffering in the same hell as you were, they will be so grateful that you have shown them the way to a panic-free life.

I cannot tell you the number of people whom I have known for years, but I had no idea they were living with panic attacks until they saw me conquer them, only then did they tell me that they were suffering and asked what I had done that was so effective for me.

## The Do's

Do let your disordered belief go

Do find a new focus

Do meditate daily

Do visualize the new you daily

Do let it go

Do educate others

## The Don'ts

Don't be a victim – don't blame complain or justify

Don't talk about panic in a negative way

Don't accommodate it, don't live your life around it

Don't feed the fear

Don't focus on what you don't want

Don't research symptoms

Don't expect other people to "make you better"

Don't visit doctors and therapists for an answer

Don't let fear hold you back, remember that's just resistance raising its ugly head

Don't become entrenched in your own disordered beliefs and opinions, this will limit your ability to see things from different angles and find new solutions to problems

Don't keep telling yourself the same old story of how unwell you think you are

# Family & Friends

This short chapter is specifically written for your family and friends to read, it will give them an understanding of how they can support you, there may be some tough love in this chapter but please understand that everything I tell them here is for your benefit.

Family and friends, I know it's hard for you to see your loved one suffering from panic disorder, but you need to understand that you can't make them feel better, there is absolutely nothing you can do about how they feel during a panic attack, everything they are feeling is coming from inside of them, and only they can take the steps to stop it forever.

However, there are several ways you can help to support them, first and foremost please try to be understanding, panic attacks can be very frightening and overwhelming, and if they see you getting wound up and annoyed, it can be very unhelpful, and upsetting for them. It is equally important not to make a judgment or criticize them for how they feel.

You can also encourage them to practice daily meditation and offer to do it together or look at finding a new hobby with them to give them a new focus.

The main thing that you can do is to remind them that they are absolutely safe and well and that what they are experiencing are just feelings, and nothing can hurt them, direct them back to this book, and remind them that they can deal with this, all by themselves, once and for all.

Do not help them accommodate the panic disorder, if you support them in adjusting their lives to avoid the risk of having a panic attack, then you are just adding to the problem.

If you would like a fuller understanding of panic disorder, then I invite you to read this book, this will help you understand what your loved one is going through.

# Troubleshooting

Below are some questions I have been asked when I've helped people in the past.

Q. How do I know it's worked for me?

A. You will know when you feel it's you who's controlling the panic attack, when you see that you can control it, then your mind no longer feels the fear of it, and therefore won't panic.

Q. Will the panic come back?

A. No, when it's gone, it's gone. Your mind can't argue with what it's experienced.

Q. What if it doesn't work the first time?

A. It will work the first time, as long as you recognize that it's you who is controlling the panic attack, it will disappear. I understand that you may be scared the first time you try this, if that's the case then take your time and do it with the next panic attack, but as soon as you feel yourself controlling it, it will disappear and never return.

That's it, you're done!

From me to you, well done!

Now go and get your life back!

# A message from the author

As I mentioned at the beginning of the book, I am not a writer and this is the first book I have ever attempted to write, but it was so important to me to share this with you and everyone else who suffers from panic disorder, I hope that you can understand and implement this easy process and have peace from panic attacks for the rest of your life.

I hope the content and structure of this book are as clear and helpful as possible. If you do have any comments or feedback please leave a review, I really would appreciate it.

I will personally read them all, reply where I can, and use your feedback to make improvements to the book for the benefit of future readers.

Thank you, and much love to you all

Kiera Scott

Printed in Great Britain
by Amazon